T0290798

HUMAN
INTEREST

HUMAN INTEREST

Valerie Bandura

Black
Lawrence
Press

www.blacklawrence.com

Executive Editor: Diane Goettel
Book and Cover Design: Amy Freels
Cover Art: "Brian T Moynihan" by Elizabeth Harney

Copyright © Valerie Bandura
ISBN: 978-1-62557-974-4

All rights reserved. Except for brief quotations in critical articles or reviews, no part of this book may be reproduced in any manner without prior written permission from the publisher: editors@blacklawrencepress.com

Published 2017 by Black Lawrence Press.
Printed in the United States.

To Patrick, Michael, Anthony, James, and Irving

Contents

SORRY, WHAT YOU'RE LOOKING FOR ISN'T HERE

The scorched town—broken columns and, dug into the earth, the hooks of the little malevolent fingers of old women—seemed to me raised aloft in the air, as snug and chimerical as a dream. The crude brightness of the moon flowed down on it with inexhaustible force. The damp mold of the ruins flowered like the marble of opera seats. And I waited, disturbed in spirit, for Romeo to appear from the clouds, a satin-clad Romeo singing of love, while a dismal electrician in the wings keeps a finger on the moon-extinguisher.

—Isaac Babel, "Italian Sunshine," trans. Walter Morison

TICKETS TO THE
GREATEST SHOW ON EARTH

Ka-Boom

I have a post card of a circus midget
with a flap in his corseted costume,
and inside is a little white dog
on a makeshift shelf, hiding
the way some say there is a god
in each of us, whatever that means
since what I hide is straight up sick,
so I half imagine this dog has his own door
and inside is an apple with a fly
sucking on the rind, and that fly has a door,
so you see how it goes, an endless
maze of chambers and alcoves
like the S&M club whatshername
dragged me to one night
when we were so young
we thought we were brave.
The Bowery, as it was then called,
a steep, dark descent of steps
to a red-lit bar and a vampire bartendress
who pointed to a man in a harness
licking the boot of a woman, dog-collared,
and further, a giant black cage
for a dangerous bird, but inside
a man bound from head to foot
in leather, gagged and drooling
and reaching through the bars
for me to release him, I mean
to release me from what secrets
and lies I tell the people I trust
never to lie to me, compulsions, obsessions,
perversions, all that pent up inertia
erupting in a cataclysmic cloud
like the great and silent force above Hiroshima.

Rodeo Good Stuff

I'm following a truck with a gun rack
and the bumper sticker reads, *Take the Migrant
Out of Immigrant*, and I think
I'm an immigrant. I think
of the time José forgot Shangxin's name
and called him foreigner,
and I said, I'm a foreigner
then laughed on the inside, but José
laughed out loud *bahaha*
because he thought
I was in on his joke. Once,
a young woman on a bus
shot up the aisle
to get a better look at my face
before asking, What ethnicity are you?
But as I told her, I said
on the inside, I'm American.
I run red lights, tail old ladies,
honk at texters while texting.
I have four American flags on the roof of my car.
How many do you have?

Halloween Burlesque

The first guest at our costume party was Hitler
on the arm of an Auschwitz prisoner,
her Twitter handle in place of a prison tattoo.

Then came Kim Phuc, the napalm girl,
in a wet, white t-shirt on which she wrote *Hot Bod*.
But we knew we had something

when the Statue of Liberty showed up
with a red Deported stamp on her forehead
since she never officially made it to shore,

followed by an executive order
that claimed on the inside
he'd known since birth he was always a bill.

What's funny about satire?
I asked Lenny Bruce
after he'd tightened his tourniquet. And he said,

How else to make sense
of the senselessness we can't take?
Okay, Rumi, I said, is it satire

if Michael Phelps swims away from shore
faster than his world record
but still drowns in a tsunami?

It is, said Lenny, if that Indonesian tidal wave
crashed Hollywood parties
so press-starved celebrities

would have to host countless galas
to raise enough money for the American Red Cross.
As for me, I went as an American Airlines stewardess,

a sliver of lip liner where the throat had been slashed,
then convinced Patrick to go as a postal worker
so he, like Santa showering guests with gifts,

could hand out envelopes with white baking powder
that sprayed from their torn seals.
What surprised everyone was Cheryl,

the toppled Saddam Hussein statue,
who turned out to be strangely less funny
than the wheelchair-bound legless private,

who wouldn't let anyone else
roll him from the drinks to the hors d'oeuvres,
and no matter how drunk he got

wouldn't reveal where he hid his real legs.

The Biggest Baby Ever

...with a baby's cry that sounds more like a lion's roar.
—*Daily News Writer*

America, you big baby, hurray
for being the least-loved celebrity
on channels you can't pronounce
in places you won't dare go, famous
for being the freakishly loud
yet none the more valid
pronouncement of you.
Your terrible cry induces
instant lactation from nipples
that shouldn't leak milk
as you pound your terrible fists
on this round little rock
while we look around, being like,
Do we just shake the baby, or
do we pacify it with tax breaks
for either the middle or upper
voting class depending on
the trickle up or down theory?
There, there. Never mind
those killed to birth you,
or that there's no breast
large enough to feed you. Tomorrow
you may lose what cuteness
attracts others to you, or
at this rate you may be undone
by your own hand, and that
would be very un-American of you.
But that's not today, this very moment,

which is the only moment we love,
since nothing has happened
so anything can.
Are you ready—
We've baked a cake and lit the candles,
and those without allegiance
to the bipartisan effort of the baking
or the candle-lighting group
have smuggled in a pop star
to sing Happy Birthday
to us, I mean you.

Cheese

You're in a bar, a bandstand, a barbeque,
with forty of your new best friends,
your first love, your next lay,
and someone with a camera says, *Cheese!*
so you slide cheek to cheek,
flash a peace sign, a gang sign, the middle finger,
and pucker in a posed posture that says,
I'm with you, but it's all me, baby,
the irresponsible babysitter, the pregnant grandmother,
the felon, the pervert, the hot mess
in the reality show I film
in a desperate darkroom of the mind
where I'm the director, stage hand, makeup artist,
who will one day, at the right angle, with the right lighting,
get my big chance, my lucky break, and then
bugles will sound and cannons will fire
as the largest volcano on earth will erupt
to cover the land with new land,
and that land will sprout a forest
in the shape of my name, teacups
will find their saucers,
pen caps will find their pens, and at dusk
a swarm of starlings will sweep and swoop through the sky
in the shape of my name, and my darlings,
I'll be the first to tell you
that when I make my big splash
I will never die.
I've bleached my teeth, sprayed my tan,
extended my hair and lashes
since anybody can be a superstar
and I'm so anybody I know it's me.

My mom, my kids, my husband
insist I'm special, a winner.
I just need to prove it
to one more, one more, one more.

The Price is Right

When Drew sweeps his hand across the Price is Right stage
toward the shimmering panels that reveal
what the announcer confirms is *A new car!*,
Drew knows the contestant opening her mouth
to let rip one distressingly loud yowl
even Drew must step back to give it room
to expand and time to release screams
not in joy, for joy has the ease of an exhale,
but this, motivated more by hysterical adrenalin,
is panic. And Drew, too, knows
from her fidgets and shakes, her maniacal
hopping from foot to foot,
that what he's looking at
is her fear of that panic. And when
the contestant recedes farther inward,
forgetting the date and year, her name
and age, unresponsive to Drew's cues
coaxing her to get a move on
stage right or stage left, only to
raise her hands to her face to salvage
whatever smidgen of pride she has left,
Drew sees there her shame of that fear.
Because what's really at stake
for these folks, folks like Drew once was,
dishwasherless folks and jet skiless folks,
is not the chance to spin the ticker-tape wheel
or land a spot in the Showcase Showdown
—among the unapologetically American
glitter and glitz of winning and losing,
girls in high heels, Drew's own bleached teeth,
and an endless electronic dinging of bells,

what's at stake is this exact part,
this grotesque public display,
an aimless, endless expression,
half dance and half flail of gratitude
for the luck they knew they always deserved,
and at the same time, an admission
of how pathetic and desperately ordinary
that luck really is, is, for the folks watching
at home, the real show—a true spectacle.
Drew knows this. He knows it so well
he pinches his mic even tighter to quell
what I can imagine must be a disgust
muddied by pity—a rancid combination
of arrogance and self-hate at the knowledge
that, let's face it, each contestant year after year
will go home to record the show when it airs
so later on birthdays and holidays
each can narrate to family and friends
how I jumped from my seat when I heard
my name, and here I come down the aisle
waving my hands, and there, that's the bar set
we could have had, and wait, here's where
I guess the wrong price, and here's where
I'm bawling as I can't find my way offstage.

The Real Millionaires of Kardashian County

When the Kardashians talk
at once at each other, I hear an aria

to the first-person pronoun, an icon
as sleek as the four-inch stilettos

girls wear to class where I teach, teetering
like skyscrapers in high wind. But hey,

when I cheated on my ex with his ex,
I, too, thought I deserved

an access to rival my actions
so I traded my wedding ring

with diamonds the size of salt crystals
for a ring with diamonds the size of capers

that glisten like a fountain in a desert
in the town where I live

that shoots ninety feet in the air
each hour for ten minutes straight, the geyser

a man-made mirage of potency
in a parched landscape of strip malls,

asphalt and extended cab pickups
with wrap around decals of the American flag

driven by cowgals with French tip full sets
who pump through subwoofers an operatic gluttony

so loud the raised veins on the blue rubber testicles
hung from the hitch of her 4 x 4

pound with such pent-up, patriotic arousal
even my blood runs red, white, and blue.

Tickets to the Greatest Show on Earth

Hands down the best Busby Berkeley rendition
was the Freddie and Fannie hearings aired on TV, so exact
even the brass eagle on the American crest
craned his neck for a better view
when the congressmen asked for the truth
about what really happened,
and who was to blame, was it you?
as each CEO covered his mic to whisper to his lawyer
as if twirling in front of his face an umbrella,
which cued that lawyer's umbrella
to whisper to his, and that lawyer's to his,
a row of hands covering a row of mouths
synchronized in a delicate arc
that cued the stenographer
to raise the pedestal of her Dictaphone,
a chrome pole she wrapped her leg around
and she was doing it and doing it, uh huh,
as the large eye of each news camera
lined up in the back stared
with voyeuristic titillation at
what ladies and gentlemen was
the greatest show on earth,
artistry of such grand illusion
we fell hard for these guys, who
hey, were just caught in a mess
of bad choices, and how irresistible
are bitter mistakes and regrettable failures
no deathbed amends could set right?
Why, these guys, they kick, kick, kicked
their painted, pointed toes,
singing and dancing and laughing,

like it was the easiest thing
anyone in his place could do.
What a skill. So in return,
we raised our hands and clapped and clapped for more.

The Gold Standard

She was right, you know,
the liberty lady on gold coins
peddled on late-night infomercials back in the 80s
when everyone, even pets,
had portfolios of so much easy money
we sipped money, then peed money,
then made plans for the money
we had yet to make. But then
comes this half-naked chick, torch lit
with the fire of foresight
to save, hold out, hang on.
How lame, we thought
in our Simple Minds t-shirts and acid washed dreams.
Now that gold's worth more than money
and half my street's in foreclosure,
Now what—do we cry?
Let's cry together. Let's join heads
to make a lake of tears.
We'll call it The Great Sob Lake,
develop some houses around it
cheap enough where all
who didn't invest in gold can live
without the fear that one day
some guy will come to our home when our kids are outside,
pat their heads a little too rough
and ask where dad is.
The kids will point to the garage,
and the man will straighten
and head toward the sound of soldering.
The sound will stop,
the adults will talk,

and when the man leaves, the notice he brought
will sail to the floor
and our kids will stop playing for good.

Rain Dance

…5,000 dead blackbirds appear to have fallen out of the sky.
—ABC News

What if, instead of dead blackbirds
falling from the sky in Arkansas,
sardines in Honduras, toads in France,
it rained money, universal paper money
from God or heaven or the Pope himself
in a flurry of praise to bless our heads
with what we know we could be
but fear are not worth.
Instead of words from the mouths
of my son's teachers for behavior and penmanship
like Super or Wow, wads of money
arranged in the shape of a star.
Instead of Thank You cards from students,
I learned so much. Money.
No hugs from my husband,
no wags from the dog. Mo-ney
to give us real faith
that someone cares—
I'd go to church then.
Hell, I'd convert—
become a bride of Christ.

Bad Joke

Hair clippings, shavings, whole locks
are flying in by the crateful
from barbers and wig stores, salons and groomers
so volunteers can stuff the legs of pantyhose
to absorb the oil in the Gulf.
I get it, the sludge
pluming from the hole we made
is a literal black mess
for the figurative blackness we're made of,
and now we're trying to plug up, clean up,
purify every last bit like a baptism
to become what we aren't,
and to do that, we'll go so far
as to cut ourselves to pieces
to make up for that part we can't.
It's penance, Yom Kippur, the Torah
we shred and keep in a box on our heads
while we wrap the arm strap tighter
to wail at the Wall. I understand.
Like the time I slept with my sister's husband
then called her up, bawling
with regret, confessing—before I told her
how he drilled his dick into me
so hard I yelled, Pump it, tiger—
I'm fucked, literally.

Head

One girl says to another, Dude,
which is a problem of gender,
I only give head to get head,
which is a problem of justice,
a song and a dance sung and danced
by women I'm sure they never saw
in the Virginia Slims ads from the 70s
who had me fooled that We've come
a long way, baby, as long as
the answer I got about sex
from my mother, her potato slicer
stunned into a stillness so terrifying
I gave up and walked out
and into a time two decades later
when my friend said, With your hand
make the sign for *Okay*
and into the hole slide his shaft
and with the fingers
nestle his balls, and I said,
Who's going to nestle my balls,
who's going to make a hole
where my frailty can hide,
which is the song and dance
of both justice and gender
I'm noticing more girls perform
with their bracelets, the ones
twelve year-olds wear,
the pink and orange ones
like candy around their little wrists
saying how far they'll go
so everyone knows in advance, so it's clear

where everyone stands when we're singing
and where when we're dancing,
so we don't mix up
who's doing who
and for what.

The Bigger the Orgy the Better the Party

How many showgirls Tiger Woods banged
is not the story. We know
they had stretch marks like tire tracks
and medallion-size nipples the color of gooseberries.
What we want to hear
is the real story behind the story,
the real mess in real time,
if he took long or looked into their faces
for help being the man
he wished he could be, or the man
he knew he should be
which are different men
in the man who can't help
but be neither. Frankly,
what's interesting about him
is how I may be popping my pimples
while you may be covered in wrinkles,
or you dig guys while I'm into girls,
but we can still get it on
under the American quilt of conflict
and comedy, united by the principle
that his fame can be our fame
and his cock our cock
screwing every square inch of this gigantic fear
we can't seem to shake
that one day we won't be
in his story or each other's
unless we make ours the one story
we can't wait to hear.

The Sweetness We Give Strangers for Free

You know why communism failed—
because it's hard to make men
play nice. Outside my office
a guy bathed in a fountain,
scrubbing his beard with what water
his hands could hold, grunting, Ah Christ
with each lap, and another guy
said to his phone, Yeah, man,
he's doing it right now. But I
did not climb into the water
and with my sleeve dab his eyes
like I cleanse my son's
because I know what happens
to those who stand up for others—like grass
grown too tall, they get cut.
Why was Avrom disappeared, you ask,
Because he said something he shouldn't have
was the answer Russians gave
when no one came back
from whichever godforsaken gulag
they went. His wrists wrapped in fur,
my Viking son stabs the microwave
with his plastic sword.
It's Halloween. Kids are working,
opening their small bags of hope
to adults ready to fill them
with sweetness we don't give strangers for free.
My son says he wants to kill someone
and steal their money. Is that right? I say.

But half an hour later, he's tired
of playing bad guy, growling at babies, scaring
princesses, and back home
has pulled up a chair in the driveway
and from his own bag
gives candy away in fistfuls.

America's Pizza

Nobody knows like Domino's,
says the voice over on the pizza commercial
aired all day, every day
in the year of bad news. Nobody knows
how to make you forget
the job you can't keep
the house you can't either
the tax money gone
to someone richer, better
looking, nobody knows
like Karen from Marketing
who's pinned an actual domino
to her lapel, how clever,
and Brandon the chef
who looks into middle-distance
when reading what appears to be
the words of real complaints
though filtered through his trained voice
sound a tad less desperate,
less true grit and more film noir,
less Honey Boo Boo and more HBO,
with a *Dirty Harry* twist,
cuz we real, but not that real. We promise,
cue the Stars and Stripes Forever,
like your boss and your bank,
to deliver on our promise.
Fade to the pizza box.
We're America's pizza, your pizza,
pan the melted cheese,
a full serving of outrage
stuffed with indignation,

on a thin wisp of air
that costs us nothing
but means the last shred of dignity
zoom in on the bite,
to you and you and you.

Mama Money

This tax season I pledge my allegiance
to taxation without representation,
or according to your tax bracket,
representation without taxation, since, man,
we all need to make more money
from what money we make.
Sure, I'll open my checkbook
to the routing number in the bottom left
followed by my social security number
which is neither secure nor social,
the number of children in our household
as opposed to the number of adults
who are not, the number of pills
we take each morning to make sure
we keep both straight, the number
per day or per week or per month
I screw for how long or well
because I understand my patriotic obligation
for full disclosure, my national duty
to maintain liberty and justice, I get
that we piss on the same fire,
douche the same vag. Sure, I believe
in a nation of love and money
as long as love and money serve all
burn outs, fuckups and hasbeens
who dance for their paychecks
from sunup to sundown each day
including Sundays as Mama Money,
the poorman's version of Mother Liberty,
mascot for the tax place in the strip mall
by the Wal-Mart parking lot

in her mint green, velveteen gown
and foam crown, her yellow sign
flipped and tossed over her head
saying *Income*, welcome, come in
you cashless shits out of luck,
miserable rock bottoms. Alight unto me.

Oh Say Can You See

When Whitney Houston sang it
        to a football stadium full of believers
in Reagonomics ready to invest
        in her money smile, her honey voice

ascended the scales of our anthem
        with the athleticism of the Dow Jones, and our flag
was a dollar bill
        sipping mutual funds through a money straw

poolside a pit of money
        where Goldman Sachs dipped his hand in cool bills.

I don't know who sang it the next year
        since the flag I flew
was a K-hole so deep, each bottom so false,
        I barely got out.

        But when I did
there was Janet Jackson's nipple
        flashing us into the next millennium
when any flag but ours terrified us.

But this year, when Beyoncé sings it
        in her leather and lace bodysuit
of contradiction, I'm at a Super Bowl party
        where the moms squabble over guacamole, the dads

circle a pig under a pile of coal
        someone spent a long time burying
so deep no one cares
        what the flag means

because no one's singing
      about fighting for a land free
of high interest rates and foreclosures
      because we're still trying to brave midnight attacks

of the Big Mac. We're still a bunch of dumb kids
      picking our noses and wiping the snot of our idiocy
on the walls of our dried up savings accounts
      and drier retirement plans,

calling our portfolio manager, our financial advisor,
      the tax guy, the pool guy, the president,
consulting the priest and the rabbi,
      the mailman, the nanny,

in search of someone, anyone
      who can help us out
with which hand is right
      and where is the heart.

NOBODY'S CRAZY.
AND EVERYONE IS.

All Points Bulletin

We all said the assailant looked nothing like anyone
we'd ever seen. In fact, we weren't sure
he was a man, certainly no man
to live around here. But, it turns out
he was and he did
and that's what we feared,
that one day we'd flick on the tube
to see ourselves on the news with a gun
loading all those shells, the shell
we hoped we'd never become
and the shell we nevertheless turned out to be,
the shell of disappointment and the shell
of regret, which are hollow shells
that go on making a sound
when the whistler has stopped,
and the shell of resentment,
which makes no sound at all,
as if all those shells loaded into twin barrels
of stickittoyou and letemhaveit
could make whatever went wrong right.

There's Always a Gunman

There's always a gunman
in the plane, at the movies, at your daughter's school,
and someone's crying, Help, or, He's got a gun, or, Fire!
It's not funny—the gun
is real, and he
means business. Yesterday,
an attendant unlocked the double doors
to let me out of the intake room
which she unlocked into the hallway, then
more locks to the lobby, until
in the parking lot, I threw into my trunk
the duffle with your coiled belt
and turned to see a face in the glass
that looked not unlike my husband's
who looked up *carbon monoxide* and *garage*, then
took the time to find the link
to erase the online history
and made the choice to hide from me
what you had planned. I shouldn't be
in this place, was what my sister said
when they put her in the hospital,
and, I was never like any of them,
when she got out. Nobody's crazy.
And everyone is. Last night,
I crept out of bed
so as not to wake our son asleep in mine,
his lips parted to a darker knowledge,
took half a pill to help me sleep,
then another after that, until
I had so many, I woke in *his* bed,
the curtains drawn, lights on, past noon,

our son by then naked in the yard.
There is a gunman,
is what I think our son would say
had he the words of this poem
with which to speak.
He'll do what it takes
to shoot the whole town down.

While You Were Out

No more each night does our kid
slip on his flying V rock star guitar
and pump the two chords he knows,
not since you got the idea
to lie back for a carbon monoxide nap
in a car you let run in the garage,
knees drawn like a fetus
adrift in a fluid of exhaust,
then got scared and gave up
the idea to give up, and traded
your belt and laces for pills
in paper cups and paper slippers.
                No,
while you were out, our son
closed his knees into a little bed
for the body of his guitar
so he could study its wound.

With his bowed head, he was a pietà
gathering into his lap the man
he was trying to wake into song.
And I was a pietà
dressing and feeding and petting
what was left of our son.
The hospital was a pietà
holding you in its pharmaceutical arms,
the drugs were your pietà
forgiving you,
                and you were a pietà
looking into the face of what you had been unable to
to understand what you had done.

The Fall

The problem is
we watched
as it happened

how could it get worse
and then did

when would it end
and then didn't, the fall

happened to us
as if we
were the actors

live and unscripted.

Hear Me Out

But I already went for coffee, says my sister
to the voices in her head that demand she get coffee

because she thinks they can hear her
as well as she can hear them.

Why don't you tell them to stop, says her phlebotomist
as he pricks a rosebud from her finger

to measure the damage done by the meds
meant to quiet the voices.

Say, Go away, he tells her
to tell them. But I have, she says,

Why won't they listen?
I'm screaming at them, she says,

and still they don't hear a word I say.

Between Me and Crazy

When I hear in my head the words
you've said your voices call you in yours

while you're dialing the phone cunt,
counting change slut, peeing whore,

I hear the words in your voice say
what I begin to imagine

you say to yourself about me
for staying away all these years,

bitch in the greeting card aisle,
freak pulling a tissue from a box,

and I want to phone you
to hear your actual voice

answer me when I ask,
Did you say something?

but you're no place where there are phones,
weaving a potholder, a dreamcatcher,

or swallowing a flower of pills
the attendant hands you

in a paper cup, careful not to
touch your hand in the exchange, or

look you in the eye, or
offer one simple nod, and

you're about to say something,
I can almost hear it.

JC Loves the Gays

I didn't call my father on Father's Day,
but I did see the JC Penney ad
with the two gay dads
wrestling with their kids
on a wool slash rayon blend sofa and accent pillows,
the kids shrieking, No no, but not really
since who wants dad to let go?
The last word I said to my father was Time,
as in, Keep it to yourself next time, after he
across a table as wide as America
at a dinner meant to give thanks
to a bounty forged by enemies, said
he's glad my son didn't turn out gay
because at school a kid punched my son
and my son told the teacher
and I said, Good job, and my father
said, If that were my kid,
I'd teach him to hit back. Screw you,
wrote username iammad
online in response to the ad
while PerfectWorld wrote, Fags are people, too.
It's about Time, how much it takes
to change and how little we have. Maybe
if I buy my dad some throw pillows
from a department store named after a god
of forgiveness, he and I
could beat each other with them
until I'd sing help help
and he'd chuckle, Oh, no you don't.

Holy Manure

The the.

—Wallace Stevens

There is no one truth, says the dreidel
to the ornament lowered from the tree
like Jesus from the cross only to be
wrapped and later resurrected.
There's your truth, says the rosary
to the mezuzah, its sacred parchment
wrapped like the shoulders of a rabbi
rapt in song. And there's my truth,
says the challah to the wafer
held in the belly of the monstrance
held in the hands of the priest
whose body is held in prayer.
There's the truth of my son's childhood
crashing my I Don't Serve Any Man party,
though here I am, bed made, milk poured, socks paired.
And there's the truth of motherhood
as I pour cup after cup of water
to cleanse the soap from his eyes
as he shrieks and flails, naked
with the truth that neither he nor I
can stop the harm that may one day be
his manhood, and what will he do
without me then? A fear so loud
I'm stunned into a silence
where I imagine the screech of shrapnel
that when it lands splinters and peppers
the soft, helpless face of a man
who, despite being nowhere near home, returns

in this moment of harm to his boyhood,
to a stillness inside a prayer
inside a ringing, which may be
the truth of manhood, but for me
is also the truth of motherhood.
What man does to man
is the truth of cruelty and kindness
which are not the same, unlike
weeping and song, which can be.
But the truth you may not have heard
is the one of the missing menorah
the lady at Walgreens promised to show me
as she guided me out of the holiday aisle
of Santa snow globes and gingerbread house kits,
past the restrooms, which is everyone's truth,
past the manager's office, past the water fountain
and payphone, and pointing at a pile of plastic bags
says, Here's your manure,
its hot irrefutable truth burning from the inside out.

Pants on Fire

Every kernel of corn, each cob in each row
are the same in a field on a Hollywood set
where a father in a commercial
sponsored by the Corn Sugar Council of America
explains to his daughter
that as far as the body's concerned
the sugar from corn
and the sugar from cane
are the same, the way
God is the same as the lamb
is the same as Hashem. And though
JC gave sight to a blind kid
and speech to a mute man,
—I learned at Mass with my in-laws
who believe in all sugar,
bear claws and sweet rolls with glucose
no natural syrup can produce—Jews
still don't believe
God is the same as a man
no matter how metaphoric
the gesture of blindness and sight
as written intended to be,
said the priest as if to me
as I sat in the first pew in church.
Thanks, I thought. I thought
God can't tell the difference
between the Jews and JC-lovers,
the bombers and the bombed.
And then my son was born
and it turns out shellfish
are neither shells nor fish,

and the body can't tell
because at his bris, the rabbi
leaned over me as the mohel
snipped my son's foreskin
to assure me that when my son
is old enough to know the sugar of a woman,
his body apparently, thank God,
will be unable to tell the difference.

Well Happy Easter to You Too

Oh my gosh, I now say,
my goodness, because my boy,
who never wore a kippah
or stepped foot in a church,
thought he'd help me out when he said,
Mama, you can't say God,
because some kid from camp
who dresses up on Sundays
and bikes door to door in a tie
looked my kid in the eye and told him
he can't say a word he heard from me.
That boy may as well have shoved his fist
down my son's throat to save a word
he thought should be set free
from hell, its wings released
toward God God God God God.
This spring, three thirty-foot crosses
with purple scarves one day stood
in a field by the church down the street
where previously they hadn't.
What's the deal? I asked
my Catholic husband. Easter,
he told his Jewish wife.
Jesus Christ, I said.
And he, Exactly.

Mom Face

Can't curl your stache or raise your thang?
The Baywatch lifeguards you hired
to serve as eye candy for the pool party
not doing it for the guests? Aw.
That's bad. Time for the Mom Face,
the frown of consternation, the pout
that says I'm sorry, but not really. No,
you didn't lose your kid
in a custody battle, or hit
a cyclist in a drunken blur.
Your mom wasn't deported.
No gunman shot up your kid's school.
A surgeon wants to break the bone
away from my friend's eye sockets
to give her the slim chance
of saving her sight. So she found a healer
who, as he explains it, will widen
her cranial plates to make room
for her eyeballs which he claims
will recede, albeit crookedly,
one looking up, one down,
so she can see
but not read or write or drive. But you,
you had an oopsy, an owie, a booboo,
the general upset
that warrants a Mom Face,
the sympathy I give my baby
who pokes his eye with a pea
meant for his mouth.
Don't cry, baby. There, there.

Make Up Your Mind

Do I run or dance
in platform sneakers?
Am I hot or cold
in Ugg boots and booty shorts?
I tell my husband it's on
on the washing machine,
then push him aside to sort through the whites.
Is whole milk in my latte
a treat or a fattener?
Does checking my son's work
make me a Tiger mom?
To the Catholic kids
I grew up with, I was a Jew.
But to Jewish kids, I had no
Hebrew name. To Americans,
I was a Commie, Say something
in Russian, they'd say.
But to Russians, they can't make out
through my American accent
what I say. Say something
in Russian, they say.
I'm leaving my husband, a friend said
in my ear as all three of us
got seated for dinner. Then
when I withdrew,
filled my lack of response
with, I don't know—you know?
But I don't know
what she didn't. Perpetual doubt
our only certainty,
you know? I don't know,

maybe I should try
the Halston one shoulder on
one shoulder off look,
the sexy mom, the MILF.

What a Peach

Real late at night, my child asleep,
two cones suctioned to my breasts,
I listen to the serenade of my breast pump
wheeze, What a peach, what a peach,
to the beauty queen in me
heading straight out of town
on her float called Where's the Party
in her rhinestone leotard as bright as a searchlight
scanning the night for trouble,
waving bye-bye to the playgrounds and preschools,
bye-bye to the mommy-and-me playdates
of this Podunk town called parenthood,
in search of a place where she will forever be
the envy of women who aren't mothers
hooked up to their breast pumps, and men
who see her and think something entirely different,
but still having to do with fruit,
an unbelievably pink tenderness
inside the thin peel
each one of the sperm they'll ever have,
balled up like ammunition,
is ready, just ready to tear.

Baby BJ

In his first weeks,
his want of milk frantic,
I saw in my son's mouth
at my breast, the red areola
raise with each lap, the tip
of the nipple toughen,
my mouth on my husband's cock, I
the man for the first time,
slumped back, eyes shut,
the milk as if marrow
drawn up and out,
that white life.

Bat City

One with a toy guitar, the other drumsticks,
my husband's putting our son down
for the night with a face-warping, fist-pounding lullaby
called Bat City
about men coming to your town
they aren't fooling around
to eat bats and suck bat blood
channeling Black Sabbath that blared from Trans Ams
squealing past our school
in a cloud of heavy metal dust.
When it settled, there we were,
a bunch of kids on the sidewalk
circling the word Ozzy
spray-painted in white like a shrine
to the rage that wrote it
the year Reagan told Gorbachev
to tear down the wall, and Soviet kids
were coming home from Afghanistan
in coffins, a discord absent now
from the rhymes in the next room
where they're getting ready for bed
by scorching whatever's not charred
with the turbo of their anthem
because what used to scare us
now puts us to sleep.

SORRY, WHAT YOU'RE LOOKING FOR ISN'T HERE

Between You and Me

I've always liked the circus freaks,
the Mule-Faced Woman and her purple birthmark
that consumed her face year by year
like a leather mask, or the twin
inside a twin with an extra cock
on the right cheek of his ass
he trained to piss on cue.
Why, it seems like yesterday
we saw Kenny Easterday, the little trooper,
pushing himself and his half spine by
on his skateboard with his hands,
or Al the Giant who fell in love
with Beatrice the Half Girl, who,
by kicking into the air her absent legs,
did handstands on what they call her fin arms.
No matter how bad we had it,
or how hard it got, they were the freak show
we could count on to have it worse.
Now they're everywhere, these amputees,
at grocery stores and pharmacies,
clicking down linoleum aisles
atop their adjustable crutches
or holding the door for you after a leak.
And they think—worse yet,
everyone lets them think—
they're just like us, sit in the same theaters,
watch the same moves
with us. So many they hold meetings,
Above the Knee Amputee Support Group,
and next month there'll be a parade
down the center of Main Street, the schools

send kids home with yellow ribbons
so we can salute them, so we can
raise one of our two whole hands
to our foreheads and look them straight
in their unbandaged eye—well, where
is the thank you in that?

Tell Me Something

Just fucked is the new look
on the runway, a disheveled detachment
originally en vogue after the release
of a grainy film from the Western Front
of boys crawling out of trenches
with bayonets in their fists
and photos of sweethearts in their pockets
ready to become heroes or men
but became neither and dropped into mud
and blood, stink and rot, gaping holes, shattered bones,
whole heads blown off. Sixty thousand
in three minutes. Absurdity
is banging your head on a wall.
But what if that wall is one of four
in which you're standing—
you're *in* the room, you *are* the party.
What are you going to play? Punk rock,
chirps my son from the back seat, and why not
the song of randomness and reverb
my hair once sang
after having done exquisite things
with anonymous men
for no reason but ruin. Why look in
when you can look out? Look out! I said
to the girl texting while riding her bike.
But she didn't hear, two earbuds
firing off a random succession of beats
in rhythm to thumbs tapping an inaudible code
of numbers and letters for words.

Too Much Muffin Top

Ohemgee, says the girl in the checkout line
at the headline of the celebrity divorce
less than a week after the wedding.
If only she read the smaller headline
of kids gassed in a Syrian air raid
or the pilot set on fire in a cage.
Did she miss the one about the White House
playing footsy with a blacklisted country
or red light, green light with our rights?
It's hard to see how desperate the disaster
for the rows of M&Ms and Almond Joys
under the rag mags
under the real news.
Am I distracting? I ask my student
who's texting while I'm talking
to him about his work.
I read online how a pregnant woman
got pregnant, though it's unclear
if she or the fetus
carry the new child
though maybe what happened with her
happened to the octogoat, a news link
that brought me to another freak story
of a goat absorbed by his twin
so was born with eight legs. At the coffee shop,
a guy's got his smartphone plugged into his minipad
snapped onto a keyboard charging an iPod
so he can text, talk, and pic
with his hands, elbows, and toes, and blow his nose
and swallow his woes. Before my kid,
I couldn't find pants small enough. Now,

I'm like the lady on Oprah
who first used the term muffin top,
and Oprah said, A what?
and the guest said, You know,
what hangs out when there's too much.

Would You Like Cheese with That

A child with no Happy Meal
whines, But I want it, to her mom
who has no Chanel bag, But it's so cute,
to her husband who wants a new Jag.
One long *Please* sung in endless rotation
from a heart with a marketing hole
what we fear and want widens,
cars to make us cool or Coke to make us smile.
My son wants a bear for his bear
and a phone for that bear
because both phone and bear
are stamped with the logo
of his favorite video game.
Or I'll die, is what he says
down on his knees,
his palms clasped in prayer
as if having once given him life
I have the power to save him from death,
though what he knows of death
he's seen on TV. But I fear
he'll one day strap an AK-47 to his back
and shoot up a Walgreens
for not filling the meds
the ads tell his psychiatrist to prescribe
for his anti-social behavior. I know
I should have a Zen palace
at the center of my being, that breath alone
aligns the chakras. But who has time
to sit cross-legged with each Big Mac attack? I don't
want to be uncool or unkind.
I want toys to stop selling my kid

the idea that pink is for girls.
I want less windows that reflect sky
and more sky. I want to whine less
and sing more two all-beef patties
special sauce lettuce cheese as I had as a kid
with Maureen and Molly and barely there string
strung together by a blind resolve
to deliver our bodies one by one
from the school blacktop
into a space between two ropes
where no one else could enter
unless they knew the words.

Salmon Fishing on the Machohanna

I have never been fishing in the Susquehanna
—Billy Collins

What I love about the Gap
is when my husband comes home in a t-shirt the color of lip gloss,
and I say, Nice blouse,
he says it reminds him of fishing the rapids,
standing knee deep
like an anchor of masculinity,
casting his strong, endless rod
into the waters of middle age
to wrangle with no less virility
what he'll later, chest heaving and arms bracing,
slice through to the meat of—
a tenderness as pink
as the girl inside him
he's been hunting all his life
who tells him when he's done, bent over
in defeat, that it's okay
to cry, to fall, to fail, to flail,
and then ask for help
and then to take it.
Because he's not fishing the Machohanna.
He doesn't even eat fish.
He's a guy who's okay
wearing a salmon shirt
to accentuate his skin tone
to look radiant and youthful from the inside.

Because I'm Worth It

How long have men been staring at blondes
instead of the direction they're driving?
As long as girls have been throwing
what they call dying parties, part
hair color, part mani pedi
to bring them *to* life, a kind of
I'll do yours if you do mine sinuous knot
of curlers and cuticle scissors.
Why wear makeup, I ask
my students, and they
sing a song of self-expression.
Then I ask how many do
when they do laundry?
Gotcha. But this morning
I brushed on blush called Orgasm
and mascara called Too Faced
before I sat at my desk alone
because deep in my female footprint
I know it's not the girls
or their goodwill, but the gloss,
the dye, the shirt, the phone, the thing
she has that I don't to prove
I'm hip or rich or smart enough
after playing twenty times on Hulu
the crotch shot sponsored by the record label
producing the singer I've downloaded
from the newer app for the smarter phone
even my mother endorses on late night infomercials
screaming at me to call now, no obligation,
what am I waiting for, the call is free!

Money is Everything

My friend asks her phone to call her decorator
to get a budget for the window treatments
to present to her husband for his approval.
They have three fountains in the front yard,
said my son when we first pulled up to their house.
Yes, I said. Yes, they do. Because
in the corporatized bank of my heart
I too would hire a chef, a bartender, and two lifeguards,
to watch my friends' kids
at my kid's birthday party,
Because, she says, it's easier.
And then adds, You know. I know
we transferred from our savings to our checking
the money we thought we'd use
to pay one card with another,
but there the money is, still
in our checking, getting used up
by what we need to survive. Money
isn't everything, I said to my father
after I told him I planned to be a poet.
Yes, he said. Yes, it is.
My son says when he's old enough
he'll drive a monster truck to get rich,
a vision equal parts mud, metal, and money,
loud cars and large fountains, torque and window treatments,
a pleasure he buys on credit
until it's gone, spent, exhausted, and he awakens
to the homework in his bag,
his bad haircut and beat-up shoes,

and looks up at me in the rearview
to say, because I say, and his teachers say,
and the books and movies say,
Only love will make you happy.

Tweenlight

While we're on the subject of vampires,
remember the 1922 *Nosferatu*,
the black-and-white figure of desire
come in the night for the girl
who is blameless in her arousal
since who wouldn't dream
of loving a bald dead man
with filed teeth? So unlike
what passes these days for sexy,
kids with daffodil faces
who look exhausted, depleted, done
already with this one life
though by the looks of it
appear to have been conscious
of only half, and which half,
the first half, who knows,
but now want not each other
to stave off a general malaise,
or a break from the parents
who aren't around anyway
to help with their homework,
their hard on, their wet dream.
What kids these days crave
is gratification without inhibition,
dual impulses, competing storylines,
like pop and punk, milk and soy
that are not so much in conflict
as conversation with each other,
a version of what I call Fanxiety
a cross between fantasy and anxiety
distilled into a bittersweet cocktail

of I'm twelve and what do I do
with the boy in the closet fear
I fear we never outgrow,
I tell my husband
since the tween in me
still expects Dracula
to bend me over and suck me dry
when he wants me to go down,
so good, he half moans
half growls from a place darker
and deeper than either dread or death,
a place like a pit of snakes seething and writhing
with a hunger for destruction and creation,
the cruel and tender, ruthless and weak,
like a newborn who rips the mother open from the inside to get out.

Any Way You Can Get It

Apparently, ladies,
according to a woman on a commercial
aired during episodes of reality weddings,
we all need a man—and not any man,
lest women gang up
on Twitter feeds the millisecond
the commercial airs to smite
the ad execs who chances are
are men with wives at home, but
curiously a black man
who pops up like a hologram
from the stage of her smartphone
in a tie at a desk
punching buttons on a computer
linked up to a home security system
to make sure, while she's out,
the lights are on, windows locked,
husband fucked, kids fed. Yeah,
we're back there—
When was it exactly we left?

Same Diff

Sure, my students laugh at the Old Spice commercial
with the buff guy on a white horse
telling you to compare your man to him.
But they roar, pee their pants,
Simmer down, says the teacher next door,
at the old school Old Spice commercial
with a Marlboro Man guy and his Charlie's Angels wife
aglow with love. These kids
were four when the Towers fell.
Is the irony in their humor
a cruelty, or is the buffer
their irony provides
a mercy? I don't know.
A woman in Alabama
attacked her husband with a raw slab of steak
she forked off the frying pan
and *wham* at his face
which welted with blood as he writhed
on the linoleum. Was her choice
not to use a gun
a cruelty or mercy? My sister
walks into a CVS and hears voices in her head.
I ask her if anyone was there
and she says, Yes, the voices. Mercy
for her and cruelty for me?
The way she tells it,
there were three, the first voice
said she was a crybaby, the second
that she was a fool, and the third
only grunted. A mercy, right?
I think this poem's pretty good,

but what do I know—the cruelty
of talent or the mercy of having none?
The woman with the steak
took back her husband, and he her,
though he's now in a wheelchair
so she has to cook.

Me, Me, Me, Wa, Wa, Wa

Since the milk sours when the cows get upset
if the milkmaids come an hour late,
Putin has pledged not to spring
the clocks forward at the Kremlin,
where they do what they can
to get out of doing what they should.
We, too, like the tantrum
that no holds barred, shoot 'em up, bad ass
smackdown that says me, me, me,
wa, wa, wa. Big bullies
are big babies. Whining and wailing
and smacking our heavy fists
atop the skull of the earth
in demand for more milk, more time, more life
until no one is safe,
unless it's the milkmaids
who can't face one more day
with one more teat, their hands sore
and chafed from squeezing and pulling
what little life gave them, saying wa, wa, wa
to aim the unpasteurized sweetness
in their little galvanized pails,
each spit of milk saying, me, me, me
amid the muddy straw of the barn,
the swallows calling wa, wa, wa
into the rafters, and the mice
at the milkmaids' feet saying, wee, wee, wee.

FB is My New BF

I look up my webpage
and it says, Sorry,
what you're looking for isn't here.
The girl of your dreams. Wads of cash.
Your mommy. What is here
is Facebook, your new best friend.
When the story about the woman
who bit her boyfriend's tongue clean off
broke, I thought, Sweet,
and wrote so on Facebook,
but got only two likes, one from a girl
whose ancestors cannibalized,
and one from my husband
who *Likes* even wolfscapes.
It's like getting a laugh, he says
on the phone in his office
to me on the phone in mine
though we're just down the hall.
Until you figure out, I say,
that the laugh's for someone else
because no one's heard you
since no one knows you.
My six-year-old dates a seven-year-old
when he logs on to Club Penguin from his iPod
and she from her iPad
so her avatar penguin and his avatar penguin
can avatar kiss—who needs talk,
to forge feeling and story
into meaning and symbol,
a longing scrubbed in a language of light?
At the quote unquote home where my sister lives

with other clients, they sit around a large ashtray
in a courtyard, the birds singing,
and drag on smoke while looking off into middle distance,
listening to the faceless voices in their heads
quip about who's the real nut job
crazy enough to down all his meds
so as not to hear one more voice.
Hell, if it weren't for the ashtray
they'd never know what it's like
to talk to an actual person.

Not Tag But War

Before the internet, my college roommate
would get as close to the actor on TV
as she could to a human ear
and whisper the punchline
before he said it, and if she guessed right,
would pat herself on her own back. Back then,
I used the paper version of Facebook
to find my RA's number to record a message
on an answering machine the size of shoebox,
my voice in her empty room
like a lost kid stuck in a dark well
calling and calling for help. Now,
Mickey's on TV blinking at my son
who's trying to guess the circle
from four shapes Mickey's holding
to save the gang from whatever on-screen trouble
he believes they're in.
What a fool, I think,
Mickey's made of my son,
then realize There is no Mickey.
There is, however, a Bradbury story
where children imagine into existence
a virtual African veldt in their playroom,
then send in their parents
to be eaten by lions. Awe-some,
sings my student for the sixty birthday wishes
on Facebook she reads to herself
walking to her room alone.
Who knows what's real.
When kids play at the park
calling out, I'm here, come get me,

hiding behind trees, who knows
if they're playing tag or war
with their semiautomatic BB guns
and camouflage pants tucked
into their black lace-up boots
pelting each other like carnival ducks
that ding and fall down when hit
but come right back up quacking.

At This Time

Ladies and gentlemen,
this is your captain speaking.
Let's turn off the iPods, iPads, iPhones, iFolks,
and stop thinking of me
and start thinking of we,
and I don't mean the video game on TV.
Let's give our attention to the attendant
so we won't fumble for an iMask,
in case iTurbulance hits our iPlane
or scramble for the nearest iExit
to avoid being blown apart
so badly it would be hard to tell
among the iBits and iPieces
if there ever was an I.

Evil

I hear there's evil in countries beginning with *I*,
as in the domain of the self,
the house of the id, the former
an actual place, the latter
a bunch of smaller versions
of the same ruination. So I wonder
how someone could stick a sticker
like *Hate Evil* on his bumper,
then sideswipe someone else with it,
that someone else wondering,
aside from You hypocrite:
one, Doesn't doing the former
mean you *are* the latter?
and two, Does either word
mean anything? each possibility
suspended in the mind
like Evel Knievel's Skycycle
over the flattened cars below,
his stars and stripes cape
flapping with a blind certainty,
that forward momentum alone
will stick the landing. Too bad
for the firstborn, I thought
when I saw my husband in the hospital
stand hands on hips over the bassinet
the night our son was born.
I saw a new father
swoon over his son. But I saw, too,
the husband scowl at the intruder.

Lie to Me

Put two strangers in a room
and in ten minutes it's
natural blonde, top of my game,
tiger in bed. Truth is,
no one wants the showgirl
without the headdress and nipple rhinestones,
but peel off the plaster and you've got
a bench at a bus stop
too wet to sit on.
I tell my son
There is a prize inside, my students
college will save them
from Do you want fries with that?
the punch card, the paper hat.
Some days I see in my husband
the face of a mugshot,
but he says he'll be just fine
after a few days in the hospital,
therapy circles, paper slippers.
Listen, just tell me I've lost weight,
this shirt looks hot on me,
you had a great time, sincerely,
call you later, feel better,
all best, love you, good luck!

Poor Lonely Irony

Mylene pours the wine while Lauren deals
the cards, and Andie reads the question,
Santa surprises bad children not with blank,
before we slide our picks across the table
to Afton who chooses, Two midgets peeing
in a bucket, over Surprise sex or AIDS
because we mustn't wish upon our children
pedophilia or sordid death, a humor
as black as a gun barrel
she may as well shove deep into the mouth
of the child. It's funny, right
until it's sad—or true. And then what?
Where do you draw the line
between humorous and offensive?
Steve told this one for years to entertain himself:
Go to an art show, he'd say, and admire a painting
by a woman, stand back, cock your head,
and when the painter comes by, say, Did you paint this?
And she'll say, Yes, I did.
It's beautiful, you'll say. Thank you, she'll say.
And then you'll say, I'm really impressed
by your talent. Can I rub your snatch? Irony,
that bad guest at the party, who farts
and won't excuse himself, or won't
lay a napkin in his lap, gets put out
in the rain, without his keys, learning his lesson,
though the conversation inside
is so terribly witty, so downright clever,
everyone's too busy listening to the noise
of their own guffawing to have anything brave to say.

The Bandura Chronicles

When I hear my name
I don't see a ukulele on steroids,
a harp hugged at the thighs and strummed at the chest
like a date in a dark theater—
you're nervous so he leans in
with hands and tongue and which goes where
decides the sounds you make. It's funny,
when I ask for a menorah at Walgreens
and the sales girl asks if I mean manure,
all I see is yellow in the shape
of a star as large as my hand
with my name stitched in black thread,
the star sown over the heart
of my mother's mother and her mother
when the Germans, one by one,
at close range, shot half the town
in what must have taken hours,
woken babies, kids in nightgowns,
the arthritic, asthmatic, anemic, it didn't matter,
no gravesites, just a mound in a field
the other half paved and use now
as a plaza for national parades. It's odd,
when the rabbi says my name, its Ukrainian
vowels leap from his Talmudic mouth
like a row of Cossacks
to kick-dance from sunup to sundown
to the rhythm of my father's name,
which is the rhythm of the body,
the rhythm of work and the rhythm of breath
as it sows and scythes the fields,
the rhythm of the oxen that cut the land

and the hands that steady the plow.
But when I Wii box my husband,
pumping my arms into the air
as he pumps his, so our avatars
can knock each other out cold
this one time we can, this one time
I can swing at him hard enough
to knock him to the ground,
this one time he can strike a woman's face
and no one will wail or come running
but laugh and say, You got me,
this one time, my name
revs with the horsepower of every NASCAR
to zoom in 3D surround sound
on the flat screen I set up
so I can turn up the volume
when the announcer yells, Go!
and with my team jersey and cup cozy,
I can be one of the drivers
gassing the peddle, gripping the wheel, and holding on
as my name wins and wins it big.
How big? As big
as the chunk of chocolate
to peek from my son's cheek
and melt in his mouth and between his teeth
as he smiles and hugs himself
so I can get the shot from above
into the white bowl, the photograph
glued to a fresh piece of toilet paper
and that glued to a scrapbook page
with the words Mud at the Gates. Shit,
I think, surrounded in traffic by Jesus fish
eaten by the word Gefilte
eaten by the word Darwin

in the same shape, swallowed whole
by a dollar bill that would pay good money
to be devoured by a peace sign.
That's what I am, darlin', an American
with a joystick, a monster truck, and a beer hat
as payment for taking each day of my life the name Name Your Price.

Total Loser

Whatever you've lost you can get back,
the virginity you worked so hard to lose,
the wisdom teeth that made you no wiser,
the money you were supposed to have saved
but spent instead on stuff you can't find.
Heartaches can now be replaced by new hearts
and new heartaches, and they say one day
they'll restore all that lost time
you spent living your life.
But what I've lost I don't want back:
loneliness the night I met my husband,
certainty the day my child was born.
I don't want the anger I had for my parents
as I'm still working on losing
the anger my parents had.
The debt, the addiction, the criminal record,
I don't want to lose any more time
carrying everything everywhere like an iPad,
which is not to be confused with the other, feminine pad.
I love the striptease I do each day
down my own personal catwalk,
losing my sight, control of my bladder, my wits
until I get to the end a total loser,
bare-assed, barefoot, and penniless,
without the pride that scars closed
each wound I ever had.

Acknowledgments

Thank you to the editors of the following publications in which these poems first appeared:

American Poetry Review: "All Points Bulletin," "Evil," "Mama Money," "Money Is Everything," "What a Peach," "While You Were Out," and "Would You Like Cheese with That"
Cimarron Review: "Ka-Boom" and "Head"
The Gettysburg Review: "Holy Manure" and "Rodeo Good Stuff"
Mid-American Review: "The Price Is Right"
Third Coast: "Between You and Me"
Waxwing Magazine: "FB Is My New BF," "Not Tag But War," and "Poor Lonely Irony"
ZYZZYVA: "Tell Me Something" and "JC Loves the Gays"

"There's Always a Gunman" appeared in the *Honest Pint No.8* broadside series edited by Matthew Dickman, published by Tavern Books.

I am grateful to the Vermont Studio Center in Johnson, Vermont for the James Merrill Fellowship, which allowed time to finish this book.

Photo: Patrick Michael Finn

Born in the former Soviet Union, Valerie Bandura's collection of poems, *Freak Show* (Black Lawrence Press, 2013) was a 2014 Patterson Poetry Prize Finalist. Her poems have appeared in *American Poetry Review*, *The Gettysburg Review*, *Ploughshares*, *ZYZZYVA*, *Beloit Poetry Review*, *Best New Poets*, and others, and have received Pushcart Prize nominations. She teaches writing at Arizona State University where she lives with her husband, fiction writer Patrick Michael Finn, and their son.